"Savor Life"
Dianne Slade

Poet in the Alley

A Journey of Addiction and Hope

W. Bryan Hart III

Compiled by Dianne Slade

Dedication

This short book of Warren Bryan Hart III's poems is dedicated to my son, Bryan: the one who could have been, but most of all, the one who was. His father, Warren "Speedy" Hart and I loved him but probably never understood the inner Bryan who refused to live up to our hopes and expectations.

He had his own road to travel.

Bryan wrote these poems whenever the spirit moved him and he had paper and pen. He told me there were many more that have been lost during his itinerant life. Often the poems would come to me as scraps of paper in envelopes that he had used for artwork on the front and addressed on the flap side. I've included a couple of these drawings in the book. The poems are transcribed verbatim; he adamantly wanted it that way.

I feel so blessed to have had the support of my husband, Chip Slade, to make it possible to heal my relationship with Bryan during the last 6 years of B's life.

I am thankful.

Dianne Slade, Bryan's mom

Introduction

Bryan's handwritten poems, typed versions and photos of him throughout his life are presented to show that Bryan was more than the stereotypical homeless drug addict. Everyone you see on the streets has their own story, but these poems are word pictures of my son's life, his thoughts, his hopes, his frustrations and his fears.

The poems are interspersed with thoughts and memories of people who were part of Bryan's life; me, his mother; Warren, his father; Valerie, his sister; Emery, his niece; Chip, my husband; Mary, his sister's friend, Mike, his life-long friend and Patsy, a family friend for his entire life.

I hope this work will help readers see both the good and warty parts of Bryan, his kindness, his refusal to fit into society's box, his stubbornness, his athletic prowess and his unconventional and irresistible humor.

The photographs are more or less chronological, but the poems are in no particular order. Some of them are emotional and hard to read, some seem racist, yet they were his reality in the place he existed at the time. He had friends on the street from many countries and many races.

Jail is a tough place to be, and it's obvious that many of these were written when he was incarcerated for a time. I can tell you that the experience of visiting there is nothing like it's portrayed on TV. It's gritty, hard and scary.

Bryan was a survivor, until he wasn't.

Memories of Bryan

Dianne, Bryan's mom

Bryan was sure he had a purpose in life. Many times he said, "Why would I still be alive if God didn't have something for me to do?" He had a deep spiritual belief that there is more than our life on this earth. Bryan was seldom without a Bible in his possession and had two in his backpack at the time of his death.

He was a troubled soul most all his life and became involved with drugs much earlier in his life than his father and I knew. He enrolled in about 15 rehabs during his struggles with drugs, completing few. His father, his sister and I tried to support and help him the best we could but his addictions were stronger than his ability to resist the alcohol and drugs.

I know we all wish we could have done more, tried harder, understood him better, been able to give what he needed that would have resulted in the healthy, happy person who was at his core.

Bryan had a lifelong best friend, Mike, with whom he shared childhood fun and mischief, teenage angst and as many adventures as they could pack into their time together.

He loved hunting and fishing. He was in tune with the outdoors and the rhythms of nature. He had a wicked sense of humor and could make people laugh just listening to his infectious cackle.

B was the most generous spirit I've known. He taught me a lot about unconditional gifts. Many of the things we gave to him had strings attached in the hope that he would change. After his death people who knew him during his homeless years have contacted us. We have heard amazing stories of his giving what little he had to someone who needed it more than he did.

I once told him that while on a trip, a homeless man approached us asking for work, saying that he hadn't eaten in days. We bought him two big hamburgers. When I told Bryan about it, B said that we should have gotten him one hamburger and given him money for the next one since he would be too full to eat two. He was probably right. He knew about those things.

He came to stay with my husband, Chip, and me on occasion for a break from living on the streets in Houston. He would usually stay for about 5 days until the pull of being back in the familiar street life with its drug connections became too strong. He worked for us and earned a little money, which he mostly used for drugs I suspect. Bryan was always a good worker when he got a job. He could hold things together for a few days, a week, but rarely longer than that before he no longer showed up. That was his pattern.

He worked around our house laying rock trails through the woods, building terraces, making steps on steep slopes, tending the garden, planting, trimming and clearing cedars. His efforts changed the fabric of our landscape so much that I see him everywhere I look.

He spent time with us on the porch in the evenings where we talked and laughed and reminisced. I will always be grateful for those times.

We did a lot of healing of our relationship out there.

When his long time partner, Deborah, died in January, 2016, he was devastated, lost and more alone than ever in his life. No matter how stormy their relationship, and it was, he loved her and she was his anchor. I believe his hope died with Deb.

Bryan was beaten to death on a street in Houston on March 30, 2016. EMS was able to re-establish a heartbeat so that when Bryan died he was able to be an organ donor.

It was his final gift.

I hope that his poems will serve as a portion of his life's purpose. He was in favor of sharing his thoughts in hopes that it may help someone else who is struggling with the dreadful disease of addiction.

I believe he would be surprised by how much his family and friends miss him and grieve his loss.

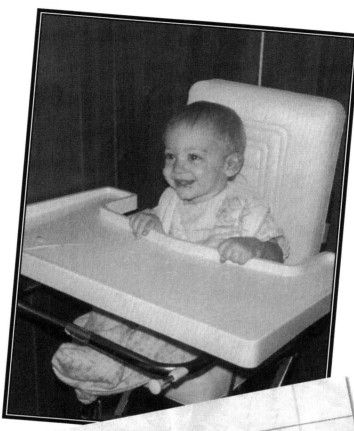

Life

Love Life with all you're heart and soul,
even when it doesn't seem to love you back,
forgive life when it wrongs you, for even Life
isn't perfect, accept Life for what it is for it
accepted you the day you were born, celebrate Life
every day even though it only celebrates
you once a year, experience the new things
in Life Because life is full of experiences
Savor Life because you're down to you're last one.

Life

Love Life with all your heart and soul even when it doesn't seem to love you back,
forgive Life when it wrongs you, for even Life isn't perfect,
accept Life for what it is for it accepted you the day you were born,
celebrate Life every day even though it only celebrates you once a year,
experience new things in Life Because Life is full of experiences
Savor Life because you're down to your last one.

Every day you wake you always have choices to make
will you do whats right today or will you the other way
or will you simply float along not doing what is right or wrong
Like leaves from the highest tree floating down aimlessly
Will you barely skim the surface or dig deep to find you're
Purpose will you try you're best to succeed and still remain who u are
for those who are in need will you go the extra mile for Diamond rings?
do you take pleasure in the simple things or must you help someone who's feeling sad
or do you find good from the bad to simply think the Lord and Pray
Do you take time out of you're day to simply think the Lord and Pray
thanking him for all you have Life's enough you should be glad
Never take the Lord for granted for you're the seed that he has planted
on this earth to grow and flourish trust in him and he will nourish
These choices are for you to make If the Lord Lets you wake

Choices

Every day you wake, you always have choices to make
Will you do what's right today or will you walk the other way
Or will you simply float along not doing what is right or wrong
Like leaves from the highest tree floating down aimlessly
Will you barely skim the surface or really dig deep to find your purpose
Will you try your best to succeed and still find time for those in need.
Will you go the extra mile to still remain with a smile
Can you take pleasure in simple things or must you have the Diamond rings?
Do you find good from the bad or help someone who's feeling sad
Do you take time out of your day to simply thank the Lord and pray thanking him for all you have
Life's enough you should be glad
Never take the Lord for granted for you're the seed that he has planted
on this earth to grow and flourish
trust in him and he will nourish
These choices are for you to make If the Lord Lets you wake.

Time to LOVE

The time to love has come at last no time for hate that time has passed.
It's time we all love eachother one another and not just youre sister father or mother
But the homeless man out on the street with no one to love and nothing to eat, the orphaned child
who hasn't felt love and has some real doubts that Gods up above lets open our eyes and all
pay attention the things that go on we don't want to mention — we all must agree that It's time
to start to get rid of the hate and put love in youre heart but until we do that it will stay like this
and we'll toss through this world and the message we'll miss that we're all here together to love one
another and not just youre sister father or mother!

Time to Love

The time to love has come at last.
No time for hate, that time has passed.
It's time we all love one another
and not just your sister, father or mother,
But the homeless man stuck out on the street
with no one to love and nothing to eat,
The orphaned child who hasn't felt love
and has some real doubts that God's up above.
Let's open our eyes and all pay attention
to the things that go on we don't want to mention.
We all must agree that it's time to start
to get rid of the hate and put love in our heart.
But until we do that it will stay like this
and we'll rush through this world and the
message we'll miss:
That we're all here together to love one another
and not just your sister, father or mother.

... replaced by presence and freeing my
... mind from negative emotions and actions that have
been programmed in my mind, accepting the good and bad in life
as equal is the way to experience the peace of life

positive energy flows through my body sending chills down my spine
as the possibilities of life awaken in my mind the failures of my
past are but a distant puff of smoke on the horizon fading
into the blue sky above In my darkest hour I saw the light
that led me to the river of hope from which I drank until my spirit
was once again full of peace and contentment
warming my soul like the sun on a cool autumn morning
and the realization that life is on time and I was early relaxes my mind
and frees me of past mistakes.

Positive Energy

Positive energy flows through my body sending
chills down my spine as the possibilities of Life
awaken in my mind
The failures of my past are but a distant puff of
smoke on the horizon quickly fading into the blue
sky above
In my darkest hour I saw the Light that led me to
the river of hope from which I drank until my
spirit was once again full
Peace and contentment warmed my soul like the
sun on a cool autumn morning and the realization
that Life is on time and I was early relaxes my
mind and frees me of past mistakes

My mind is Locked down, unable to cross it's boundaries Longing to venture out into the unchartered Territories of itself ~~yet it~~ far away from the Mundane routine of my ~~daily~~ existence

Time ~~seems is~~ frozen yet it ~~melts~~ melts away in the blink of an eye Leaving tommorrow in Puddles of memories that I step in today

Time

My mind is locked down unable to cross its
boundaries Longing to venture out into the
uncharted territories of itself far away from the
mundane routine of my daily existence
Time seems frozen yet it melts away in the blink of
an eye
Leaving tomorrow in puddles of memories that I
step in today.

Memories of Bryan

Valerie, Bryan's sister

My brother, Bryan, lived his life without concerning himself about what was to come. While this proved unbelievably frustrating for me and my family at the time, I now see the beauty and freedom in living your life this way.

Bryan was a total pain in the ass to me for most of my childhood. He was the bad kid in the family and I was the good one, able to get away with much more than I should have. He loved to bug me, it cracked him up. I don't think he ever got tired of irritating me, right up until the end.

When his drug use began to escalate in his late teens and it became clear that he had a real substance abuse problem, I was scared for him. Scared of the possibilities that this drug use would lead to if not controlled and he was unable to get sober. I still find it hard to believe that my fears were realized.

Not only was I scared for him, I was truly scared of him and of the way he behaved when he was high or drunk. He could be so wildly happy one moment and uncontainably angry the next. His behavior could not be predicted.

Bryan was also one of the kindest, most generous people in the world. When sober, he was thoughtful and unbelievably compassionate. He would give or do anything for someone he felt was in need. I see these traits in my children and am grateful that we shared some of the same genes.

And he was funny, damn funny. Without a doubt that is what I miss most about him. We shared the same sense of humor and I miss this bond we had more than I ever imagined I could. He and I basically have the humor mostly attributed to a pre-teen. We would laugh at wildly inappropriate times, a really bad singer at a wedding, for example. When my husband accidentally bumped a lady on a motorcycle in a parking lot, Bryan and all of my kids were in the car. Bryan and I could not look at each other for fear of cracking up. Awful, I know, but the lady was fine.

He was able to mimic others in a way that would leave you in stitches, with facial contortions, mannerisms and hilarious voices. It was the best.

Bryan loved me and my family so much. I have regrets that I was not more accepting of this love before he was gone. He really truly just wanted my love, acceptance, and just my company so many times and I pushed that away. I am not sure if I was trying to "fix" him or whether I was protecting myself, probably some of both.

I still have trouble wrapping my brain around the fact that he was homeless. The reality that he sat on street corners hoping for a dollar and slept in alleys is so unbelievable and so painful, especially for my mom.

Even though these were his circumstances, he was part of a community. He had people he connected with that witnessed the good in Bryan, people that knew him and loved him. For this we are so grateful.

I will always and forever miss him.

Ready for Peace?

I'm ready for peace and I know you are too
So let's all do our part and make it come true
Lets accept one another for just who they are
and their religious beliefs whether they're near or
far
Let's take a few minutes out of each day
to serve someone else and go out of our way.
Let's open our eyes and help those in need
and focus on them and not our own greed.
Love is contagious and it won't bring you down
do your best everyday to spread it around.
So let's <u>all</u> do <u>our</u> share and start to look in
and not look at others for where to begin.
Love's the Solution and Now we should start
and it will catch on if we just do our part.

Awakening

In the Hour of my awakening the world sleeps soundly
and time is frozen reminding me that the days screaming in my head is the voice of silence
reminding me that the days list past as my mind becomes clear
the clouds from the horizon of my mind I see a world of
opportunities ahead of me and a lifetime of lessons behind me
the realization that we are all one of the same on this earth
is the missing piece of puzzle that completes the picture the many questions of life
far to see the world for what it is I must look within myself
and not at the world i

Awakening

In the Hour of my awakening the world sleeps
soundly and time is frozen solid
Screaming in my head is the voice of Silence
reminding me that the day is past.
The clouds clear from the horizon of my mind and
I see a world of opportunities ahead of me and a
Lifetime of lessons behind.
The realization that we are all one of the same on
this earth is the missing piece of puzzle that
completes the picture of Life
for to see the world for what it is I must look
within myself and not at the world.

...that God is calling me to him
... right outside my door the choice is
Dear I open it all I see is Love then
all the years of pain & hurt fly away
on the wings of a Dove,

                    Amen.

Change

The time to change is chiming loud
I've heard the sound before, I never knew those
other times just what the sound was for
I've wasted way too many years with drugs and
alcohol, the Lord has tried to pull me up, but I
would always fall a slave to the Devil's ways for
way too many years
All the pain and agony sometimes came out in
tears but more than not it stayed inside festering
each day
The Devil had me in his grasp I couldn't get away
But once again I hear the chimes and know what
they are for
I finally hear what I could not for many years
before that God is calling me to him
He's right outside my door the choice is clear
I open it and all I see is love then all the years of
pain and hurt fly away on the wings of a dove.

Amen

but how long will it Last? But only God knows
the day so until then I'll sit and pray for my release
from this Hell I cant wait to hear the freedom bells
Ringing Loudly Just for me when that day comes
I shall be free from the Hell that I've Been
living Because Jesus saves and he's all forgiving
my sins and my past the good times are here
at Last

Awake Again

Here I lie, awake again wondering when it's going to end
Trapped in a cage I'm all alone, a feeling I have seldom known.
But not like this, not this way, God I dread another day in this cage all by myself I feel as if I'm on a shelf
Put up here and forgot
Left up here to spoil and rot
My mom won't see me, she won't bother I must remind her of my father
But I won't dwell on the past, I'm still in jail, how long will it last? But only God knows the day so until then I'll sit and pray for my release from this Hell
Can't wait to hear the freedom bell
Ringing loudly just for me when that day comes, I shall be free from the Hell that I've been living
Because Jesus saves and he's all forgiving of my sins and my past
The good times are here at last.

Threshold

My time is up and just begun as I cross the threshold of imprisonment to freedom, stepping out into the world I am born again only this time with a smile, my interpretation of Life takes on new meaning as the doors to my mind have swung wide open and reality stepped in. My compassion for others and passion for Life itself is the fuel that ignites my hope for the future and lights the way to my dreams.

as I sit   dejaVue

~~sitting~~ here alone in the cool of the shade
the breeze stirs up ~~the~~ memories that have
settled in the Back of my mind of younger days
filled with time to kill, ~~and~~ before
time began to show signs of killing me,
This sudten *flash back* ~~deja vu~~ is a frightening reminder
of just how short a Lifetime is
yet at the same time it seems as though time
has not ~~passed~~ yet passed

Déjà vue

As I sit here alone in the cool of the shade
the breeze stirs up memories that have settled in
the back of my mind of younger days filled with
time to kill, before time began to show signs of
killing me.
This sudden flashback is a frightening reminder of
just how short a Lifetime is.
yet at the same time it seems as though time has
not yet passed.

Memories of Bryan

Patsy, family friend

Memories of Bryan will not be forgotten as we were best friends of his parents. Through life you have many ups and downs but we all like to focus on the good times (many of which we had). Our families and friends spent many a weekend hunting, fishing, barbecuing and just good times doing family functions with all our kids.

Bryan really loved his family, friends and parents and God knows they loved him. We are all saddened by the death of Bryan but we do know he is at peace in the hands of our loving God.

Words to describe Bryan: Protector, Caretaker of friends, Private, Unique Individual, Warm Gentle Heart, Bro, True Friend, Faithful, Tenacious.

Note from Dianne:

Our families were close for many years and shared times at the South Texas hunting leases and on the coast for most of the lives of our kids.

Once, on the way to the lease, Bryan and Jennifer were fighting and hitting each other in the back of the car.

When they arrived at the lease, Bryan's dad took him aside and said, "Bryan, you don't hit girls!"

Bryan looked at him in shock and said, "Jennifer's a GIRL??"

It has been a family joke ever since.

This is a picture of Bryan and Jennifer roasting hot dogs at the lease.

NEW DAY

Waking up from the nightmare of my life I thank God to of made it out alive
relief wraps its arms around me as I realize it is over
And the sobering reality of life is a gift I'll continue to cherish forever
my eyes see the clarity of the world in a new light and my soul
heals the heart beat of Love for the first time this cold hard world
we walk through is a play ground compared to the night mare of my past
And my future is but a mountain I've already climbed the pitfalls ahead of
me have all been filled in with the knowledge of my past
my futures as fresh as a new day dawning and the wind is at my Back
Blowing me in the right direction!

New Day

Waking up from the nightmare of my life I thank
God to of made it out alive
relief wraps it's arms around me as I realize it is
over and the sobering reality of life is a gift I'll
continue to cherish forever.
My eyes see the clarity of Life in a new light and
my soul hears the heart beat of love for the first
time in this cold hard world
We walk through what seems a playground
compared to the nightmare of my previous
existence.
The pitfalls that lie ahead of me have all been
filled in with the knowledge of my past
My future's as fresh as a new day dawning and
the wind is at my back,
Blowing me in the right direction.

Surrounded by his Panics
his Panic grew more every time
he would hear the guard open the door
one more his Panic Just added to
his Panic Musta been 40 of them
N only one a him / Tone change
He could feel thier glares and thier
cold hearted stares he just Looked up
and hoped to Hell that God would hear his
Prayers

but the b
life through Jesus ↻
Lord."

Roman

Panic
(written as a song)

Surrounded by his panic
His panic grew more every time he would hear
the guard open the door
One more his panicin' just added to his panic
There musta been 40 of them 'n only one a him
(tone change)
He could feel their glares and their cold hearted
stares he just looked up and hoped to Hell that
God would hear his Prayers.

Road to the future

Alone with my thoughts we sit in silence remembering the past for it is now I build the road map to my future, yet the pot holes of my past are now marked with a detour sign. ~~~~~~~~~~~~~~~~~~~~ in my mind, and the bridge to self destruction ~~~~~~~~~~ has been burned. my thoughts turn to the future but momentarily stop in the present to reflect on the roadmap of my past before I move forward again, turning right into the future, the road is clear ~~~~~~~~~ and along with my mind, Hope is riding shotgun for the first time in a long time and the trip has just begun.

Road to the Future

Alone with my thoughts we sit in silence
remembering the past for it is an invisible road
map to my future, the pot holes of my past are
now marked with detour signs in my mind, and
the bridge to self destruction has been burned.
My thoughts turn to the future but momentarily
stop in the present to reflect on the road map of
my past before I move forward again, turning
right into the future, the road is clear along with
my mind.
Hope is riding shotgun for the first time in a long
time and the trip has just begun.

the ones who have so much dont care about the rest
the ones who have the least will
share it with the rest I dont know   Blow Down
what its going to take to Bring   well just remember
the world together But I know if   you'll Be Judged
we dont try were in for rougher   when you're layed
weather Jesus said to treat each   to rest
person as they were himself
But I dont see that happening from   EnD
the ones w/ all the wealth
they must think that they're to good
and only want the Best

Slow Down

The ones who have so much don't care about the
rest.
The ones who have the least will share it with the
less.
I don't know what it's going to take to bring the
world together.
But I know if we don't try soon we're in for
rougher weather.
Jesus said to treat each person as if they were
himself,
But I don't see that happening from the ones with
all the wealth.
They must think that they're to good and only
want the Best.
Well just remember <u>you'll</u> be judged when you're
layed to rest.

End

Memories of Bryan

Mike, Bryan's friend

I met Bryan in 2nd grade. We were great friends. He was always at my house early in the mornings in the summer and he always got called back home to do chores. We would ride our bikes for hours, far from our house as young kids. We would go to McDonalds and Baskin Robbins (Bryan loved the Rocky Road) then we would go to the bowling alley and try to rig the machines for free games since we just blew our money (that was usually the change from Speedy's (Bryan's father) change jar.
I remember Bryan and I being mean to a lot of kids -- Lee, Jeremy, Allen, Trace, and B.J. to mention a few -- the list goes on. We were Bullies no question.

It took a lot for Bryan to talk. But when he did he would lay down the facts. He disappeared to school in Maine and I would get a phone call now and then. He ran away couple times and we hung out for short times. We crossed paths at a rehab In Dallas called Straight where I was a counselor and he just came in - Weird - I was brain washed. I miss him. This is tough.

Bryan was Very Smart- I know he walked in on our friend Cliff when he had a shotgun in his mouth- Bryan had to talk him out of it. Bryan had bite marks on him from fighting people that 99.99999 percent of the people in this world wouldn't even have the courage to look in the eyes.

Bryan would always give people nicknames and loved to make funny faces. He was a very giving person. He dated Beverly (Bevo) and Silvia and Debra.

He used to ride the bus all day in his later days just to keep in the AC. He would sleep in the woods and get free chicken from Churches every night at closing time. He made great friends with a lot of people at the bus stop and was a very genuine person. He was a great salesman.

Bryan was Very Very Very Close to God. I believe that's what kept him going.

my mind has been robbed of sleep once again and the thieves are long gone
my eyes travel the room as my mind travels the memories of my life
the night passes by in slow motion while my thoughts are in fast forward
and it feels as though the sun may never rise again
the seconds take minutes to pass and the minutes hours!

Void

My mind has been robbed of sleep once again and
the thieves are long gone.
My eyes travel the room as my mind travels the
memories of my Life.
The night passes by in slow motion while my
thoughts are in fast forward.
The seconds take minutes to pass and the minutes,
hours.
And it feels as though the sun may never rise
again.

but every day comes and every day goes and be...
keep it together I say it again they're all on my nerves I just can't take this
I'm sick of their voices and tired of their faces in my mind I travel to distant places
But I can't stay gone too long as you see the noise never stops they won't let me be
my blood is just boiling I want to explode my brain has been sent into overload
I could kill em all but not fast enough and I sure would take pleasure in
doing it rough If I had one cookie some one would want half
But keep it together is what I must do and so I will try
until my time is through.

Keep It Together!!!

"Keep it together", "be patient and wait"
these are the things that I say everyday
but everyday comes and everyday goes
and with each one past my anger just grows.
"Keep it together" I say it again.
they're all on my nerves I just cannot win.
I'm sick of their voices and tired of their faces and
in my mind I travel to far away places
But I can't stay gone too long as you see
the noise never stops they won't let me be.
My blood is just boiling I want to explode
my brain has been sent into overload.
I could kill 'em all but not fast enough and
I sure would take pleasure in doing it rough
But "keep it together" is what I must do and so I
will try until my time is through.

my thoughts ~~bounce~~ ricochett back and forth like a raquetball game being
played in my mind thoughts of the future the past ~~the~~ my hopes and
regrets ~~the~~ my fears all seemingly find my mind at once
the here and now is the same as yesterday and will be the same tommorrow
staring at the concrete walls that surround my life my thoughts
evoke emotions in my being that I ~~cant~~ cannot desipher sleep is hiding
and cannot be found anywhere the pleasures in life are burried deep
within my mind and too much work to dig out hope for the futures
but a distant star in the galaxy of my mind dim ~~but~~ yet visible
through the wreckage of my past.

Ricochet

My thoughts ricochet back and forth like a
racquetball game being played in my mind
thoughts of the future, the past, my hopes and
regrets, my fears, all seemingly flood my mind at
once.
The here and now is the same as yesterday and
will be the same tomorrow
Staring at the concrete walls that surround my Life
my thoughts evoke emotions in my being that I
cannot decipher.
Sleep is hiding and cannot be found anywhere the
pleasures in Life are buried deep within my mind
and too much work to dig out.
Hope for the future's but a distant star in the
galaxy of my mind, dim, yet visible through the
wreckage of my past.

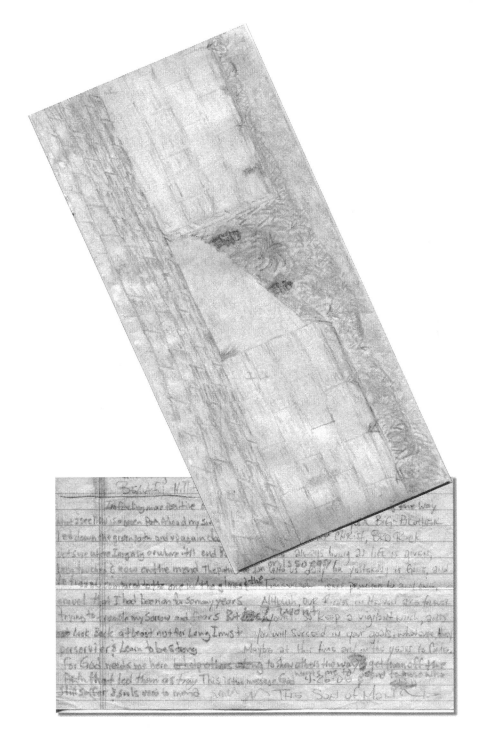

The Green Path

I'm feeling more positive every day,
the fog is now clearing, I'm seeing the way.
What I see now is a green path ahead.
My soul is now touched and I'm being led
down the green path and up again.
Down the green path around the bend,
Not sure where I'm going or where it'll end.
But my soul has been touched and now on the
mend.
The path that I'm on is so easy to travel
compared to the one with the glass and the gravel
that I had been on for so many years
trying to trample my sorrow and fears.
But I won't look back, at least not for long,
I must persevere and learn to be strong,
for God needs me here to show others the way
and get them off the path that led them astray.
This is the message God wants me to send
to those who still suffer and souls need to mend.

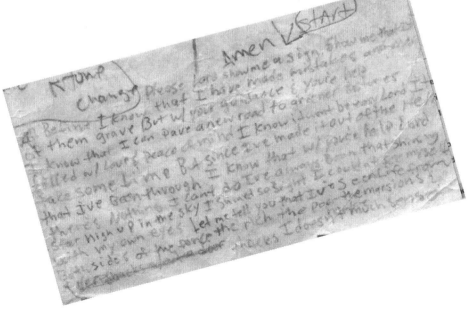

Prayer

Please Lord show me a sign. Show me that I'll be fine.

I know that I have made mistakes and many of them grave.

But with your guidance and your help I know that I can pave a new road to greener pastures filled with love and peace of mind.

I know it won't be easy, Lord.

It'll take some time but since I've made it out of the Hell that I've been through I know that with your help Lord there's nothing I can't do

I've always been that shining star high up in the sky.

I shined so bright I couldn't see myself with my own eyes.

Let me tell you that I've seen life from both sides of the fence the rich and the poor, the mansions and the shacks

It doesn't make much sense.

The Moment

At peace with the world she and I wrapped in a
blanket surrounded by the perfectness of Life
nothing matters but how the clarity of nature
seems brilliant in the dawn of the day ahead
No fears, no worries, just love and awe for this
world we live in
The earth is still as the serenity flows in and out of
our beings creating perfect harmony with the
earth around us
Time is of non-existence and the only existence is
the moment in itself

Memories of Bryan

Emery, Bryan's niece

I haven't seen my uncle, Bryan Hart, in a while. My mother's brother, he had the same warm hazel eyes, wrinkled skin, and unbeatable smile as her, yet his eyes reflected much more heartache and loneliness than he ever revealed. His frayed plaid shirt and tattered jeans hanging on his thin body, Bryan used to return temporarily into my life for Thanksgiving and Christmas celebrations, always bearing gifts, regardless of his personal debts and desires. Although my memories of Bryan are scarce and distant, they have always remained imprinted in my lower skull, like artistic inscriptions in ancient caves.

The first memory, a brushstroke of crimson red paint, reflects my first recollection of embarrassment. On one cold Christmas day, as I applied my brand-new lip gloss in the mirror, I looked up to see Bryan grinning at me. He exclaimed, "You aren't supposed to eat that!" and cackled his easy-going laugh at me (he scared me at first.). My face heating with flaming blotches, tears of naivety stinging in my eyes, I rushed past him and outside into the brisk winter morning. Of course, Bryan chased me down, wiped my tears, and made me laugh an uncontrollable sort of giggle by entertaining me with his facial contortions and impressions, hilarious antics to a child. Bryan was always one of my favorite relatives.

Dancing with the crimson brushstrokes are streaks of white, a pigment of clarity and perfection. Perfection? To me, Uncle Bryan's piano skills were nothing short of perfection, a repertoire of short, simplistic jingles and catchy tunes. For hours, he sat, cross-legged, on an itchy, wool carpet in front of my plastic keyboard (a prized possession), lending me his musical genius and encouragement. With my small, uncoordinated fingers, I fumbled the notes every time, but he made me feel like the best pianist in the world.

At that tender age, I was unaware that Bryan was a homeless drug addict. I knew that he smoked cigarettes because he always retreated to our back porch with a pack of villainous lung-destroyers. Marks of black charcoal created shadows in my memories. Time after time I would approach him, hands on my hips, and tell him with my matter-of-fact attitude that smoking is dangerous (my mother instructed me to do so.), and he would find some way to distract me from the burning assassin in his hand.

Around that time, Bryan started to bring his girlfriend, Deborah, to our family gatherings. Her dirty, crooked teeth (meth) frightened me. Although the adults seemed awkward around her, Deborah and I conversed rather naturally, and she would inquire about my childhood adventures, treating me as an equal just as Bryan did.

About 3 years later, when I was snooping around the Christmas tree, I saw a gift labeled "To Emery, From Bryan" in my mother's handwriting. When he entered the house empty-handed, I understood Bryan's circumstances much more, a burden in his dark circles, an air of discomfort surrounding his body. When I was finally allowed to rip through the sparkly, red wrapping paper, I uncovered a wallet designed of my favorite black and white floral pattern, one that my mother and I discovered together.

Of course, I exclaimed my thanks, smelling the smoke on his plaid shirt as I hugged him tightly, and I pretended to misunderstand the shame in his voice when he replied, "I'm glad you like it." Strokes of dark plum deepened my memory, reminding me of the embarrassment and isolation he felt around my family.

After that Christmas, Bryan stopped attending our holiday celebrations, and every once in a while I would interrogate my mother about his disappearance. "He's working in Houston," she'd swiftly reply. As months and years passed, I no longer noticed Bryan's absence, that is to say, until I overheard my grandmother whispering about Bryan's rehab as she poured herself another glass of wine – I knew I wasn't *supposed* to hear.

I had always been taught to vilify drug users as

animalistic, dangerous, and suspicious criminals who lack values, self-restraint, and any ounce of human decency. As an eleven-year-old child, I, sitting in the leather backseat of a luxury vehicle, witnessed my friend ask her father if we could lend a dollar to the homeless woman standing at the stoplight. The vagrant, barefoot, held nothing but a cardboard sign that read, "Anything helps." Nevertheless, her father retorted, "No, never give anything to homeless people. They will only use it for heroin." I couldn't imagine knowing someone who lives on the streets. That wasn't the Bryan that I knew.

I don't remember exactly when Bryan visited last, but I do remember the last words he spoke to me: "Stay in school because it is the best thing you can do for yourself." A middle school student at the time, with nothing but years of education in sight, I believed his statement to be the most obvious concept in the universe, failing to realize that he never attended college. Since then, I hardly talked to Bryan, and my multicolored memories faded into an indistinguishable depiction, each hue dulled by time and overshadowed by the fog of my thoughts.

Deborah died of cancer about one year ago, and my grandparents paid for the funeral. Somehow, with his staunch determination and kindhearted character, Bryan convinced a storeowner to allow him free calls, and my mother would cry every time they conversed. Enraptured in my own world, I hardly noticed her tears until last March when he passed away.

How does one react to the death of a stranger? Initially, I didn't feel much, until I saw my grandpa's swollen, shocked face, my heart cracking as I realized that he lost a son. When my older brother, Jack, hugged me, my heart cracked as I realized that my mother lost her sibling. I'm not sure how I would cope with the loss of my brother, but it certainly wouldn't be healthy.

In wake of the storm, friends visited my family to keep my mother distracted, bearing wine, baked goods, and comforting shoulders. In the meantime, I would run. I traveled miles and miles in and out of our neighborhood (searching for an escape), attempting to clear my mind and pump a cure into my heart. To find a purpose in the tempest, I filed through boxes and boxes of family photos, helping my grandpa organize a slideshow for the funeral.

Bryan looked exactly like Jack, and exactly as I remembered him. As I once again met his warm hazel eyes, wrinkled skin, and unbeatable smile, all the colors came back. The red, the white, the black, the purple. The lip gloss, the piano, the cigarettes. I couldn't believe that I had ever forgotten his devilish grin, his hilarious immaturity, or his deep-rooted kindness. Only then did I realize how much he loved my siblings and me.

At the funeral, upon my grandparents' request, I stood at the podium in front of a small crowd to read scripture, voice cracking as I uttered, "We do not lose heart...," tears choking me into violent sobs. It was the most challenging, uncomfortable, humiliating, heart-breaking experience of my entire existence, and I couldn't repeat the verses if I tried. However, I know it was something that my grandparents needed me to do, and I would try again if they requested.

A few months after the burial, my grandma shared Bryan's poetry, a collection of his letters, with me. In his words, I watched Bryan's charcoal shadows breathe life, recognizing the internal battles and dark addiction that he endeavored so painstakingly to mask. From tragic to hopeful, shameful to indignant, his poetry highlights so much of his character that he never allowed anyone to see. In the hope that Bryan's poetry will resonate with others experiencing the same heartache and battling similar demons, my grandmother is venturing to publish his words, allowing him to make a permanent difference in the world. That is what he always wanted. To help someone, to wipe their tears, to make them laugh

Now I understand his message, his life, and the mural of my memories so much more. I recognize him in some of my mother's deep-rooted emotions: her dread at the sight of tattoos (Bryan had an eagle imprinted on his upper back), her anxiety for her children's future, and her despair that no one remembers the real Bryan, the compassionate brother, the whimsical uncle, the faithful friend.

Today, Bryan's canvas gleams more vibrantly than ever before, and he has impacted me more than he, or my mother, even knows. When I become frustrated with challenging pieces of music, still sitting on the same itchy carpet, I play Bryan's simplistic jingles on my plastic keyboard. When I see homeless people at stoplights, gripping their cardboard signs, wearing forlorn expressions, I offer them a smile. When I apply lip gloss, I hear Bryan's voice and his unmistakable cackle. I will never again forget him.

Memories of Bryan

Mary, Valerie's friend:

Bryan Hart, I remember you.

You had a wicked sense of humor and a nickname for everyone. You were a keen observer of the absurd and a great mimic.

You were kind to me and welcomed me into your home like the rest of your family.

I loved to watch you with your sister. You could frustrate her, but also make her laugh like no other.

You let us girls intrude on your space. We stole your beds at sleepovers, we commandeered the couch and television and we roamed your house and backyard as if no one else mattered. You were never the annoying little brother, just a cool cat with a smirk on your face and a smart ass comment to follow.

We all move through life with the nicknames you gave us. And we will always remember you.

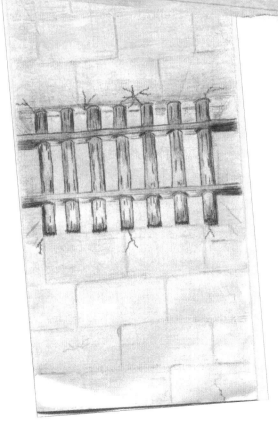

Just Another Day

It's Just another day in cell 25, my body is wasting but I'm still alive
I've been here 30 days I can seem to keep my mind in a haze
oh how I wish I was out of this cell out of this day out of
this Hell Just another day in pure misery oh how I ~~want~~ to look out
see the birds in the trees the clouds in the sky even the cars going
by but the walls here are white & my mind is grey and its getting
worse in every way the pick axe has swand from my left to my right
I just want ~~~~ to go away but I want a fight and also a sore that's on my right
of the Doctors not sure he thinks it is staff my body is worn like steel I'm
to tire its just another log of pain on the fire when will it all
end I hope not much Longer but one thing's for sure I'll come out much Stronger
So when I leave here I can honestly say life will be more than
Just another Day

Girl

Just Another Day

It's just another day in cell 25, my body is wasting
but I'm still alive.
I've lost 16 lbs in 36 days. I can't seem to focus my
mind's in a haze
God how I wish I was out of this cell out of this jail
out of this Hell
Just another day in pure misery
Oh how I want to look out and see the birds in the
trees the clouds in the sky, even the colorful cars
that pass by
But the walls here are white and my mood is gray
and it's getting worse in every way.
The pink eye has spread from my left to my right
It just won't go away, not without a fight
and also a sore that's on my right calf
the doctor's not sure, he thinks it is staff.
My body is weak, it's starting to tire
It's just another log of pain on the fire
When will it end? I hope not much longer
But one thing's for sure I'll come out much
stronger
So when I leave here I can honestly say,
Life will be more than Just another Day.

The Stranger

as he sits by the river gazing at the reflection of a stranger staring back at him he wonders where the man he once knew had gone and when he left the lines on his face are a roadmap of the many rough roads he's traveled in his lifetime and a constant reminder of his hardships his spirits as hard as the soles of his feet from ~~my~~ years of walking through a rough life and regret is his constant Compassion fear and ~~worry~~ no longer live in his mind for they moved out years ago ~~and~~ when acceptance moved in ~~his~~ only friend left is killing him slowly with each swallow he takes and he welcomes him with open arms ~~he lays down by the river and closes his eyes~~ the sadness in ~~a soft patch of clover~~ and thanks ~~the good lord his life finally over~~ his eyes ~~penetrate~~ the world and creates Confusion in a young Childs mind This man we all know we see him each day ~~yet still~~ ~~The man is the stranger~~ we call him the stranger.

The Stranger

As he sits by the river gazing at the reflection of a stranger staring back at him, he wonders where the man he once knew had gone and when he left. The lines on his face are a road map of the many rough roads he's traveled in his Lifetime and a constant reminder of his hardships. His spirits as hard as the soles of his feet from years of walking through a rough life, and regret is his Constant Companion. Fear and worry no longer live in his mind for they moved out years ago when acceptance moved in.

His only friend left is killing him slowly with each swallow he takes and he welcomes him with open arms.

The sadness in his eyes penetrates the world and creates confusion in a young child's mind.

This man we all know we see him each day still we call him the Stranger.

you'll be there one Day

you'll be there one Day IF God has his way,
Its too Late now, you dont bother to play,
you've turned a blind eye to people in need,
Now you'll lay in your filth and suffer indeed,
See it will come back, to you ten fold when
you're laying there helpless and you're body is cold,
shivering and shaking from the waste you lay in
I hate to say it but I'll have agrin, you bought you're
own ticket so you'll take the ride, see there's nothing to
save you especially you're pride, see it left you too,
the day you fell I'll Now you're asking yourself
Is this really real? you'll Reflect on you're Life and
Suddenly See, WHAt I've done to them is happening to me,
And its Just the beginning its going to get worse
you'll be all alone, and wont have a nurse, you'll
Probably lay there and wish you were dead, But God
wont Let you die you'll suffer instead
..... from you're head to you're toe.

You'll Be There One Day

You'll be there one Day if God has his way,
It's too late now, don't bother to pray.
You've turned a blind eye to people in need,
Now you'll lay in <u>your</u> filth and <u>suffer</u> indeed.
See it will come back to you tenfold when you're
lying there helpless and your body is cold.
Shivering and shaking from the waste you lay in
I hate to say it but I'll have a grin, you bought
your own ticket so you'll take the ride, there's
nothing to save you especially your pride, see, it
left you too, the day you fell.
I'll know you're asking yourself Is this really real?
You'll reflect on your life and suddenly see what
I've done to them is happening to me.
And it's just the beginning, it's going to get worse.
You'll be all alone and you won't have a nurse,
you'll probably lay there and wish you were dead,
But God won't let you die, you'll suffer instead
You'll suffer in pain from your head to your toe
To Hell you will go and then you finally die.

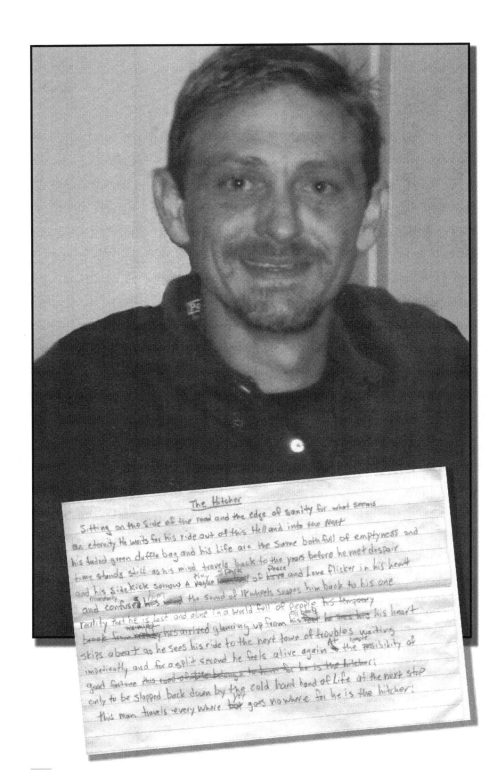

The Hitcher

Sitting on the side of the road and the edge of
sanity for what seems an eternity, He waits for his
ride out of this Hell and into the next.
His faded green duffle bag and his life are the
same, both full of emptiness and time stands still
as his mind travels back to the years before he met
Despair and his sidekick, Sorrow.
A tiny spark of peace and love flicker in his heart
and momentarily confuse him.
The sound of 18 wheels snaps him back to his one
reality that he is lost and alone in a world full of
people.
Glancing up from his boots his heart skips a beat
as he sees his ride to the next town of troubles
waiting impatiently and for a split second he feels
alive again at the remote possibility of good
fortune, only to be slapped back down by the cold
hard hand of Life at the next stop.
This man travels everywhere yet goes nowhere for
he is the Hitcher.

When the Money Ran Out

Well, when I first met her it was peaches 'n cream.
It happened so fast it had to be a dream.
Things were going fine so it seemed,
but when the money ran out so did she.
For the first 2 years it was steaks 'n wine
She was happy as a clam doin' just fine.
Then in an instant things went south.
I couldn't believe the words that came out of her mouth.
Yeah, when the money ran out, so did she,
faster than a squirrel getting' chased up a tree
I didn't know what hit me it happened so fast.
I just turned around and she was haulin' ass.
I started gettin' mad and told her to go to hell,
then I stopped and thanked the Lord
there were no wedding bells
Cause when the money ran out so did she,
faster than a squirrel getting' chased up a tree.
Now I'm all alone just me and the cat.
The look on it's face is wondrin' where she's at.
Now a few weeks have passed and I'm just fine
I got me a pretty red on my line.
Well the moral of the story, friend, is easy to find,
Make sure ya know the broad before it's steaks 'n wine.

Memories of Bryan

Speedy, Bryan's father

I know you can choose what to focus on in recalling your memories of family or friends who have died. You can choose to remember the pain and heartache they may have caused or you can choose to remember the fun and loving good times. Sometimes the difficult times seem to overwhelm every memory. Thinking of the good times makes me smile and feel good inside. Seeing old pictures of happy times also makes me realize that there were more good times than I really remember.

I especially remember how excited he would always be on our hunting and fishing trips. He was five and six years old when I first started taking him. He was a natural and learned so quickly that is was as if he already knew how. He loved the outdoors and learned quickly how to be a survivor should it become necessary. I always knew that he was so safety conscious in the field that I didn't have to worry too much. I actually felt safer around him than some of the grown men I have hunted with. One of the trips that is most vivid in my memory is a fishing trip at our home in City by the Sea. Bryan was twelve years old and was driving our small outboard by himself at that time. One afternoon he returned and announced that he had found the perfect place to fish the next day. We left at first light the next day and he took us so far from our normal fishing area that I was sure he did not know where he was going. He took us to a spot that I had never tried and there were no other boats around at all. We started catching Red Drum immediately and caught them all morning long.

We wore ourselves out and when we left there were probably twenty boats around ours. He was so proud of himself for finding this spot that he smiled all day.

That was just one trip but there were so many although maybe not as successful however, but all had great stories. I will always cherish the memories of the good times we shared on those trips.

I miss Bryan terribly and grieve the fact that we were not able to continue, as he grew older. However the memories of trips we had and all of the old photos help me to focus on the real Bryan. The person that the Lord created was a wonderful loving human being that I love and will always be proud of. I am so thankful for our good times together and that he is no longer in any pain or discomfort and is with his Lord. I love you Bryan and God Bless you.

Another Serving of patience ~~please~~

Another Serving of patience Please; Just keep it coming thats all that
I need, my nerves are en edge and my head is throbbing
What patience ~~isn't~~ just the others are robbing,
I try to stay calm and just cant to ten or think happy
thoughts Like Places Ive been I'll go there for a
minute but then I'll come back and nothing has changed
theyre still on the Attack slamming down chairs and
talking so loud of the crimes they've committed theyre so
very proud, Sometimes it is hard to look them in the eye
for fear that they'll know what Im thinking inside
that ~~they are~~ just the scum of the earth It's truly a
tragedy thier mothers gave birth to such drains on
society and doers of Wrong I Just pray to God ~~I dont~~
~~have to stay long~~ I wont stay here long,

Another Serving of Patience

Another serving of patience, please.
Just keep it coming, that's all that I need.
My nerves are on edge and my head is just
throbbing.
What patience I've left the others are robbing.
I try to stay calm and just count to ten
or think happy thoughts like places I've been.
I'll go there for a minute but then I'll come back
and nothing has changed, they're still on the
attack.
Slamming down chairs and talking so loud
of the crimes they've committed they're so very
proud.
Sometimes it's is hard to look them in the eye
for fear that they'll know what I'm thinking inside
That all of them are just the scum of the earth.
It's truly a tragedy their mothers gave birth
to such drains on society and doers of wrong
I just pray to God I won't stay here long.

She Never Left Right
(written as a song)

She never left me right
She took off outta here without a warning or a fight
Well I guess that she just got tired of my ways
But I just snapped and realized the girl's been gone for
days
Now I'm wondrin' where she's at
And why I even care
She done me wrong
I ain't brushed my teeth or even combed my hair in DAZE
That's what I'm in
I can't think of anything except where the hell she's been
I guess I gotta let her go and do just what she will
Me, I need a real stiff drink and a little bitty pill
She never left me right
She only done me wrong
But I'm tired of dwelling on her so I'll end this song.

Gods kept...
...he gets all the...
I've got to press on
...times I wished I were...
...there out of my head...

I'm getting frustrated w...
It seems never ending. I've...
but I don't see the use it's doing...
any kind of way see for yourself...
and probably will still be here tomorrow...
then and still with same sorrow. So when will... ...I ponder
until my mind grows weary and just s... ...ponders, I trust
in the Lord that he has a plan but ...am just human and
only a man I cannot forsee the future ahead for that is a
Book I haven't yet read all that I'm asking is just to be
free the mistakes I've made then I now truly see
So I pray to you Lord won't you please let me out
and I'll be a new man for I have no doubt
                        there is
And I will do all in your glorious name
So my name is still Bryan - But I'm not the same
yes I am

Frustration

I'm getting frustrated with time that I'm spending locked
in this cell.
It seems neverending.
I've tried to be patient as long as I could but I don't see the
use.
It's doing no good.
It's not paying off any kind of way.
See for yourself, I'm still here today
And probably will still be here tomorrow
More frustrated then and still with the same sorrow.
So when will I leave?
This question I ponder
Until my mind grows weary and just starts to wander?
I trust in the Lord that he has a plan
but I am just human and only a man.
I cannot foresee the future ahead
for that is a book I haven't yet read.
All that I'm asking is just to be free.
The mistakes I've made then I now truly see.
So I pray to you Lord won't you please let me out
and I'll be a new man for there is no doubt.
And I will do all in your glorious name.
Still Bryan—But I'm not the same
Yes I am.

my eyes have finally opened to the truth that lies ahead

Freedom

Looking out my window from the cell that I sit in
I'm reflecting on my past and all the ~~things that I~~ things I could of been
The decisions that I've made ~~have all been for the worst~~ in life
have not all been the best I've been run hard and put up wet I really
need a rest but rest is not an option now I've got to press on through
I must decide just what I want and what I want to do
change is what I'm longing for from the bottom of my heart
but not knowing which way to go I don't know where to start
I pray that God will lead the way and show me what to do I hope I can
~~accomplish this before my time is last my path clear~~
guide me when I'm lost and give me strength to carry on no matter
what the cost soon I'll have my freedom back and that's when I can start
to change my life for the good from my old ways I will put
~~the past start type be ahead~~ of me the days that lye ahead of me
will be nothing like my past and with my effort ~~and~~
they will last ~~so I'll leave you with~~

Freedom

Looking out my window from the cell that I sit in
I'm reflecting on my past and all the things I could have
been.
The decisions that I've made in life have not all been the
best.
I've been run hard and put up wet.
I really need a rest, but rest is not an option.
Now I've got to press on through.
I must decide just what I want and what I want to do.
Change is what I'm longing for from the bottom of my
heart,
but not knowing which way to go, I don't know where to
start.
I pray that God will lead the way and guide me when I'm
lost
and give me strength to carry on no matter what the cost.
Soon I'll have my freedom back and that's when I can start
to change my life for the good from my old ways.
I will pray the days that lie ahead of me will be nothing
like my past
And with my effort and my faith I know that they will last.

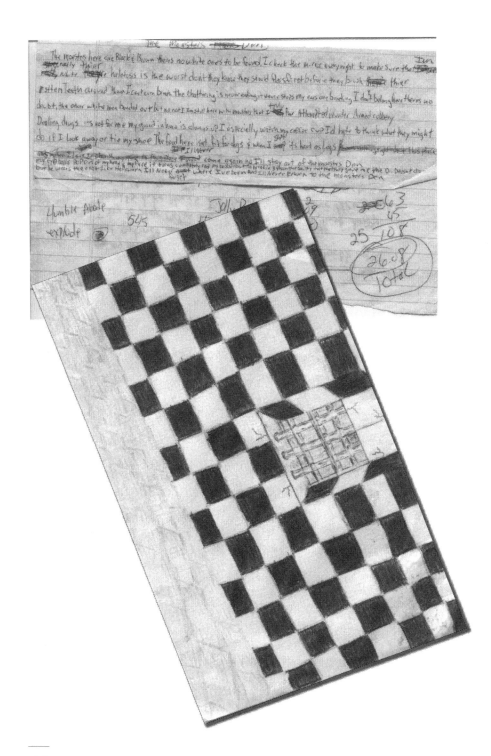

The Monster's Den

The monsters here are black and brown, there's no white
ones to be found. I check the mirror every night to make
sure that I'm really white. Their halitosis is the worst.
Don't they know they should floss first before they brush
their rotten teeth?
Around them I can't even breathe. The chattering is never
ending.
It never stops, my ears are bending. I don't belong here,
there's no doubt. The other white men bonded out
but no not I.
I'm still here with monsters that I truly fear.
Attempted murder
Attempted robbery
Dealing drugs
It's not for me.
My guard in here is always up. I especially watch my
coffee cup. I'd hate to think what they might do if I look
away or tie my shoe.
The food here isn't fit for dogs and when I shit it's hard as
logs.
I'll never come again. No, I'll stay out of the monster's den.
My eyeballs pop out of my head and my face it turns
completely red. My back's about to break in 3 from the
shitty mat that they gave me.
The Dr. doesn't do anything but he wears the coat like
Halloween.
I'll never forget where I've been and I'll never return to the
Monster's Den.

Halitosis

I'm elbow to elbow with Mexicans and blacks.
There's no other whites, so I watch my back.
Their breath is so rotten I try not to breathe
But when I finally do it knocks me to my knees
I'm constantly turning from my left to my right
testing the air for freshness.
I might, but I'm not so sure if I'm ready yet.
I know if I breathe what I'm going to get,
two nostrils full of holy halitosis.
Of all the bad breathe I've smelt this is the grossest.
Yes, this halitosis has serious power
It went through my clothes, now I need a shower.
But I cannot leave and I cannot breathe.
I'm locked in this cell and this is pure Hell.
They go on and on talking their shit
of crimes they've committed and years that they'll get.
They don't seem to care what will happen to them.
It's all just a joke, their future looks grim.
Now I understand God wants me to see
if I don't change my life it just might be me.
Minus the breath cause I'll always floss
and to lose half my teeth would be such a loss.
But seriously, the point is real clear,
If I don't change my ways I will be back in here.

Memories of Bryan

Chip, Dianne's husband

My first in-person exposure to Bryan was a result of his plea for help. Up until that time, he was just a story to me. Yes, I'd seen him at our wedding a year or so before and could see he was in rough shape even then but I only exchanged a few words with him and couldn't say I knew him. Of course, I knew most if not all of the story of Bryan's known youth, his many, many visits to rehab centers, his escapes from them, his rebellion against finding anything other than whatever path was unfolding before him, his brushes with the law, bad choice after bad choice for close to three decades. I knew of how much promise his mother felt that he held once upon a time. Her hurt and disappointment in the way his life was turning out was palpable. At that point though, she still had hopes that he could find a way to something resembling what we "normal" people thought of as normal.

We got a call from him somewhere around late October to early November. He was seemingly on the run and out of luck sleeping in a doorway in Tyler, Texas. We found a way to get a bus ticket to him and bring him to our home out in the county. Picking him up in downtown Austin, regardless of what we knew to expect, was unnerving. He looked shockingly thin, dirty and just plain hard. Obviously, he'd been on the streets for a good while. He had said he was desperate, before us was the proof of that. Thin, hauntingly gaunt, actually, sunken eyes and everything you'd expect if you had the imagination to conjure the image. Dirty, unshaven, thin as a rail, maybe 6 feet tall and probably around 115 pounds.

85

When he got here, he slept for what seemed like two straight days. Probably, he was coming down off of one high or another. I've been around drugs and some addicts in my life but I'd never seen it gone this far.

Bryan stayed with us for four months as I recall. He was grateful for the respite from the cold. He cleaned up over that time. He turned into a person again before our very eyes. I think he put on 20 pounds, maybe more over those months. He loved his mother's home cooking and she loved cooking for him.

I know they talked a lot over this time. They had some real heartbreaking and heart mending one-on-ones that, although I don't know the details, cleared up some long held misconceptions that formed in Bryan's teenaged days and colored his thoughts ever since. They bonded. He regained his respect for her and, during this time he found that he did indeed love her and that her love for him had never faded even in the darkest moments. Many tears were shed.

The timeline here is a bit convoluted but the facts are the facts. I don't think I'd ever been more disappointed in a person than when Christmas rolled around. B had been clean for a couple of months at this point. My naive mind thought he'd see now that this was the way and repeating old mistakes was so, so the wrong way to go but…he disappeared over Christmas from his Dad's and hit the streets looking for the old "comfortable to him" environment. He could be "The Guy." He sold virtually all of his Christmas presents for drugs and a hot night out. Having "stuff" never meant anything to Bryan. I'd thought long and hard before I gave him an iPod with his kind of music pre-loaded. It was the most perfect gift for anyone of all I gave that Christmas, for he LOVED music. Gone…all for a couple of hours of fun.

A couple of days later he called, strung out. His mother and I talked and we agreed that we'd give it another go...it seems we knew we were being played but it really was easy having Bryan at home. Leaving him there surely wasn't going to help. Bryan and I had a real heart to heart in a coffee shop down on Austin Highway before I made the final decision to get him back home. The thing is, you KNEW Bryan was telling you his heart felt truth about wanting to be clean and his apologies were deeply felt. He just couldn't hold on to that moment for long. So home we went. Once he slept it off, he pitched in on yard work for pocket money. Even though he's gone, we still delight in looking out and remembering some good times we had with him here.

This drug thing is a mighty foe. Even though the Christmas story had been burned in our minds, we still wanted to believe in Bryan. I guess that's the story of his life...he could MAKE you believe he was getting there then...POW...right in the kisser...he'd hit you with a repeat of the storyline. Around the end of February, he had followed our advice and saved up around a grand that would get him wheels so he could work away from home. We looked around and found an old but serviceable clean red Subaru Forester. He loved it. We titled it and insured it and soon he was off to a gift of a job from his father and brother-in-law. Did it last? Yes, for nearly two weeks. He just couldn't stand not having his old buddies and their kind of fun when they were so close. He couldn't take the loneliness of an apartment with no one there to talk to. The car was stolen, the safe life with a promising job was gone and so was Bryan. There was trouble in River City and he was off to Houston.

We saw him off and on over the remaining years. He had hopes of getting clean and getting a job but nothing much ever panned out as far as we know. There was always some reason he got fired or didn't last. Most of the time, it was someone else's fault...in Bryan's mind.

Now that you have the surface facts, try to square that with this:

Bryan really loved helping people. I don't mean a little here and there, I mean he'd give you every single thing he had knowing he would find a way to get what he needed to get by, one way or another, tomorrow. Food, clothing, time, talk…all you had to do was ask.

Bryan could read people like a trained psychologist. He didn't trust many folks and he may have well been right about that.

Bryan had a relationship with a woman we really couldn't warm up to but he loved her. They may have had a co-dependent relationship but damned if he didn't love her head to toe. Her death is really what killed Bryan. He died of a broken heart before he died on the streets from physical harm.

Fact: You do not know anyone as emotive as Bryan was.

Bryan loved his family. All of it with all he could. Yes, he scared the heck out of all of us at one time or another but you know deep down he did love you.

Bryan told me once that his mom marrying me seemed weird to him but that after we talked, he was glad she did. He said I was cool. Bryan, so were you. Maybe too cool. A lot of folks would give a lot for you to not have to fight the demons you did. You left too soon but I know you were ready to go. We'll remember your good and there truly was a lot of that.

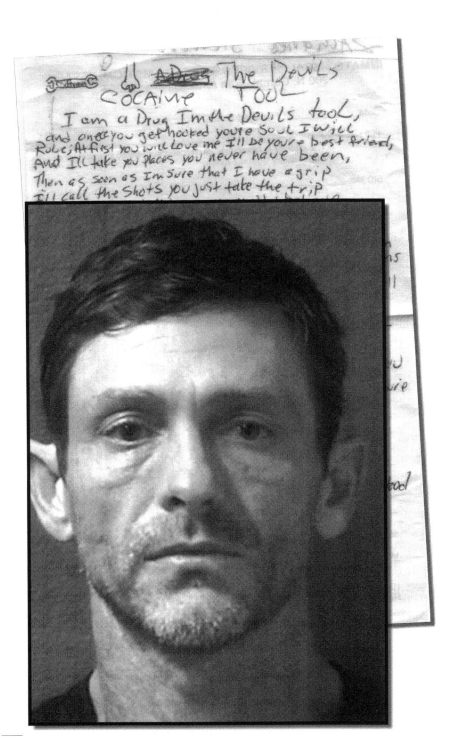

COCAINE The Devils TOOL

I am a Drug Im the Devils tool,
and once you get hooked youre soul I will
Rule; At first you will love me I'll be youre best friend,
And I'll take you places you never have been,
Then as soon as Im sure that I have a grip
I'll call the shots you just take the trip

Cocaine, the Devil's Tool

I am a drug. I'm the Devil's tool
and once you get hooked your soul I will rule.
At first you will love me, I'll be your best friend,
and I'll take you places you never have been.
Then as soon as I'm sure that I have a grip,
I'll call the shots, you just take the trip.
I'll make you do things you couldn't believe,
and though you will suffer, your loved ones will
grieve.
I'll take all your money and I'll buy you pain
and I'll leave you homeless, stuck out in the rain.
I'll take over your thoughts and actions as well.
and slowly your life will become living Hell.
I'll make you sell everything that you own,
then look up old friends and beg for a loan.
and after that's done you will steal and rob.
You must have the money but you can't hold a job
Your body's too weak and your mind isn't there
and you're realizing now that the world doesn't
care.
I'll put you in danger whenever I can
and run you in circles never having a plan.
So I'll leave you with this.
Don't be misunderstood; if you choose to use me,
I'll fix you for good.

Epilogue

Bryan was loved by so many, helped so many and had so much promise and hope during his life that it's hard to believe that he's gone.

Reading his words gives a sense that he never believed that drugs would be his end. He had faith, he had hope, and he had a vision for a future that didn't include what he knew to be a killer in one way or another. I hope you can see from the pictures of him throughout his life that there were choices made that narrowed his possibilities. There was a point of no return in his drug use saga.

Bryan was unable, for reasons I don't understand, to accept the help offered by people who loved him or by the numerous rehab units he attended over the years. He was a child of privilege. It's been said that he was one of a very few homeless people who could both scuba dive and snow ski. Drugs robbed him of his promise.

You may be in this situation…someone may be extending a helping hand and you feel unable or unwilling to reach out to grab hold of it. The way your life turns out is determined by the choices you make in every step of your life. Take one step, make one choice at a time. Bryan knew this and wrote about it in many of his poems.

I pray his words will speak to you and will reach your heart so that you see that the world is indeed a place of wonder and miracles and that there are angels ready to give you a new beginning. Reach out and grab that extended hand.

Warren Bryan Hart III
May 15, 1972 – March 30, 2016

Acknowledgements

My thanks are extended to many people, but most notable are Sean Bridges, Max Thomas, Gail Gonzales, Steve McCurdy, Chip Slade, the Dream Builders and the Masterminds. You know who you are!

Notes

Made in the USA
Columbia, SC
30 September 2017